UNCOMMON SENSE

To ~~Dennis~~ & Linda,

Enjoy each and every moment —

All the best,

Marck

Also by Marck Cobb

*Aerial Refueling: The Need for a Multipoint,
Dual System Capability*

UNCOMMON SENSE

*Searching For
Inspiration & Wisdom*

MARCK COBB

Uncommon Sense
Searching For Inspiration & Wisdom

Copyright © 2010 by Marck Cobb, Galva, Kansas.
All rights reserved. This publication may not be reproduced, stored in a retrieval system or transmitted, in whole or in part, in any form or by any means, electronic, mechanical, photocopying, recording or otherwise without prior written permission of the copyright holder.

Amosalitary Publishing Company
2160 Mohawk Road
Galva, KS 67443

                                    p. cm.
1. Cobb, Marck. 2. Self realization. 3. Leadership—Biography.
4. Spiritual life—Biography. 5. Cobb, Marck—Philosophy.
6. Ideals (Philosophy). 7. Inspiration

Library of Congress Control Number: 2010903587

ISBN: 978-0-615-35583-2

Designed by Jim L. Friesen

Printed in the United States of America by Mennonite Press, Inc., Newton, KS

*To my parents
Redell and Barbara Cobb
for empowering me with their beliefs
and
To my wife and son
Francine Liem Cobb and
Layton Redell Cobb
for their understanding, love, and support.*

Acknowledgements

This book is the product of many friendships, challenges, and life-long experiences. I am taking this opportunity to express my deep gratitude to the best teachers, relatives, students, and friends who have influenced and inspired my thinking.

I am most grateful to my brother Kinley Cobb, who reviewed the initial manuscript and offered many valuable suggestions. I owe an additional debt of gratitude to Layton Cobb and Carla Barber who assisted in the final editing of this book.

Finally, I am deeply grateful to Don Setser for his excellent photographs that are included in this book showing the pictures and sculptures that provided hope and inspiration in my life.

Contents

	Prologue	1
Chapter One:	Pictures That Inspire Me	5
Chapter Two:	Inspirational Family Roots	23
Chapter Three:	Meaningful Sculptures and Symbolism	31
Chapter Four:	Pillars of My Spiritual Foundation	45
Chapter Five:	Teachers of Wisdom	53
Chapter Six:	The School of Hard-Knocks	65
Chapter Seven:	Influential Friendships	79
Chapter Eight:	Simple Beliefs	87
Chapter Nine:	Advice for the Next Generation	95
Chapter Ten:	The Golden Years	103
	Epilogue	111

The Story of the Chess Clock

*A chess clock keeps track
of time for both sides,
his hands wave pointedly
but he has no allies,
he has no opinion,
but he rates every game,
though he ticks for hours
he gets no fame,
the chess players hit him
and smash him and beat him,
but this clock is brave
and always faces toward them,
with pride and respect
for the clock that he is,
he thinks he
has no time for this.*

—Layton Cobb

Prologue

Why am I writing this book? What purpose do I hope to achieve? Do I have time for this? In short, I am writing this book for two reasons. The first reason is to provide a written record as a small part of my personal legacy. It basically covers six decades of my life as it relates to conversations and interactions with five different generations in my family. The second reason is to provide a more detailed insight into my experiences for the benefit of my readers and as a token of my gratitude to the people who have influenced my life.

Whenever you initiate a life story, one begins with many questions. For example, what makes my story unique and worthwhile for others to read? Which good experiences or bad experiences will give hope or inspiration or insight to others? How many relatives, friends, and acquaintances does one include? How much philosophy do you discuss? Should you include stories of religion, politics, and close personal relationships? All of these questions deserve some attention. However, my intention is to write a relatively short version of a few of the more notable experiences that have occurred in my more than three-score years of life.

As a chess coach for elementary, middle, and high school students, I am constantly impressed by the creative and analytical abilities that my students achieve based on their inner motivations. I am convinced that we need to look for the good strengths in students and that we should strongly encourage their natural talents in a constructive manner. In all of my parenting, teaching, and coaching, I have consistently found the carrot approach of positive reinforcement and acknowledgement to be the most rewarding method to obtain the best results. When the best results are achieved, they become a source of inspiration for continued success.

Several of the anecdotes in my life story will describe the many carrots that were placed in front of me. I have learned that this positive motivation allowed me to confront the challenges and overcome the obstacles placed in my pathway. It took both inner motivation and external motivation to maintain my confidence to continue taking the gradual steps forward to accomplish the successful achievements in my life.

Jerry Klingaman, a university research analyst who is one of my close friends and a former colleague, told me more than twenty years ago that each of us has a story that can be written as a book. This is my beginning to fulfill his words of wisdom. It is my sincere hope that my life experiences based on faith, desire, perseverance, and fearlessness will serve to inspire others to achieve better and greater accomplishments in their lives.

Golden Wings

On golden wings I have dreamed of
 far off lands with more beauty than
  I can imagine.
Of places where
 time stands still
  as the world rushes by.

On golden wings the dreams come true,
 oceans of blue,
  hills of green.
The tallest mountains and the deepest valleys
 have been seen from afar
  and up close.

On golden wings I ride through the heavens,
 the land far below me,
  the clouds ahead.
The clear dark sky above me,
 dotted with the glow
  of far away stars.

On golden wings
 I have flown with the power
  that man has created.
Can I fly on my own?
 Will I soar above
  when my time has come?

I know I will.
 Given my faith on these golden wings.

—Jon Thompson

Chapter One
Pictures That Inspire Me

– 1 –
A Picture is Worth a Thousand Words

Throughout my life, whenever I look at a picture I usually formulate a mental impression that impacts the way I think in some way, shape, or form. We have all heard the phrase that a picture is worth a thousand words. I will try to express only a few of those words based on some of the pictures that I have collected during my adult years which have had an influence on my philosophy of life.

–2 –
Token of My Memories

When I was working on my Master's Degree in National Security Affairs, I was assigned to the Naval Postgraduate School in Monterey, California. That part of my education was both a challenging and memorable experience. I had served in the Air Force for seven years and was excited to expand my education with the opportunity of attending graduate school. I had no idea of what to expect at a school that was operated by the Navy. This was definitely another opportunity that would impact my young life. As a token of my memories of living in Monterey, I decided that a picture of the ocean and the west coast would be an appropriate keepsake.

Although I am not an artist, I have always appreciated the ability of an artist to capture the various scenes in our lives. In many of the art galleries in nearby Carmel, there are numerous painted pictures of the oceans. The problem was how to find a unique ocean picture that simply did not look like all the others.

I was diligent, took my time, visited many galleries, and

Breaking Point by Ralph Jacobs.

eventually found one unusual picture painted by Ralph Jacobs that truly depicted an ocean wave in action. It captured the sunlight beautifully reflecting and shining on a wave that was crashing on the rocky coastline of the Pacific Ocean near Monterey. Surprisingly, the artist had named the painting "Breaking Point," which could have more than just the simple meaning of waves breaking at a point along the coast.

– 3 –
Capturing the Ocean's Power

Naturally, the painting symbolized the strength of the ocean's power in a crashing wave at its very peak before it uses all of its force to break against the rocks. I spoke with the artist and met his mother who provided additional meaning about the work that was done by her son. She explained the intricacies of capturing the light of the sun on the peak of the waves. After several days and much thought, I purchased the painting. Ralph personally brought it to my home and helped me hang it in my living room.

Every day, when I look at this painting, as I have done for more than thirty years, I am reminded of the challenges we face and the breaking point when these challenges are resolved. This is a more complex and philosophical meaning that can be inferred from his painting. We all must face the breaking points in our lives. Paintings have been an invaluable source in reflecting on the numerous challenges I have faced over many years.

– 4 –
International Creativity

Another picture that gives my life meaning was painted by the wife of Gerard Gourlet, a very dear friend of mine. We became acquainted during my assignment as an assistant air attaché to Moscow. This particular painting was done as a gift to me from his wife Edwige, a very creative artist and the mother of five children. The work of art accomplished by Edwige reveals the numerous inter-relationships that exist in the everyday world of our lives. Unfortunately, my French friend Gerard recently passed away from cancer, but his memory is shared in his wife's painting.

Kremlin Church Domes by Edwige Gourlet.

As part of the gift, Edwige had explained to me that she needed a canvas which could not be found easily in Moscow. Since I was scheduled to fly to Germany, I was able to purchase some canvasses during my visit. Once I delivered the canvasses to Edwige, she painted an outdoor scene of the Russian Orthodox churches with the gold onion domes located inside the walls of the Kremlin fortress. This piece of art is truly an example of international friendship and cooperation. A painting that was created by a French woman; painted on a canvas from Germany; capturing a Russian scene; and, presented to a very grateful American. I don't know if Edwige knows the deep emotional impact of her artwork, but it provides an inspirational memory of my time in Moscow as well as our enduring friendship.

– 5 –
Eve and the Apple

Some of my other favorite pictures are examples of love, nature, religion, and friendship that were painted by my Russian art friends. One such artist, Boruch Steinberg, not only painted in several different mediums, but he also did metal artwork. During my stay in Moscow, I became friends with Boruch and his wife Tatiana Levitskaya, who also did creative artwork using primarily acrylics.

One of the paintings done by Boruch is a very fine, detailed ink-dot pattern that shows the religious symbolism of Eve coming out of the apple. Only an artist like Boruch could have the creativity within his limited freedoms

Eve and the Apple by Boruch Steinberg.

while living in the Soviet Union to symbolize his religious beliefs and not get in trouble with the government that had outlawed religion. The ability to painstakingly create this artistic statement with such small ink-dots made me fully appreciate the time it took to complete such a tedious task. The picture illustrates the understanding of religion and the perseverance that is needed to express the spiritualism of this understanding. It also illustrates the dedication to one's natural instinct of being a true artist.

– 6 –
The Look of Despair

Tatiana presented me with an acrylic picture of the facial torment of a young Russian girl looking at the open landscape of the Russian terrain. The young girl has a somewhat forlorn look of despair, which during the era of Communism and dictatorial rule, expressed the unstated sentiment of what many people who lived in Russia had to confront on a daily basis. Every time I look at this picture, I am reminded of how fortunate we are to live in a country that allows us freedom of expression without being hindered. It is a picture whose thousand words cannot be spoken verbally to express the emotions of the Russian populace. Since the end of the Cold War, both of these artists have become extremely successful in the Russian and European art world.

Russian Girl by Tatiana Levitskaya.

– 7 –
HIGH LIFE IN MOSCOW

I met another Russian artist Valeri Rudenko, at a diplomatic reception in Moscow, and our mutual respect for each other resulted in an invitation to visit his home. Valeri lived in the same apartment complex where Christina Onassis had lived while she was married to her Russian husband. During the time I lived in Moscow, artists could mingle with foreigners, but they could not become too friendly without problems from the KGB. Consequently, Valeri told me to park my car a block from the apartment when I came to pay him a visit to avoid the presence of my diplomatic license plates being too near the vicinity of his apartment complex. He would then meet me to walk to his home.

The Rudenkos' second-floor apartment was directly above a store. Valeri and his wife served hot tea and hors d'oeuvres on their patio which was on the roof of the store. The window in the second-floor apartment was the entry way to the patio, decorated with flowers and equipped with chairs for sitting and enjoying the outdoor summer evening. The atmosphere was most relaxing and the three of us could sense the trust and sincerity that was mutually shown by our conversations and actions. In this instance, the actions spoke louder than words and created a treasured friendship that will never be forgotten.

– 8 –
Children's Illustrations

Before leaving Valeri's home, I was offered some original water color paintings that had been used in Russian books for children. One of the water color pictures depicted a bird catching a fish with children playing on a boat by the water.

Children Playing by Valeri Rudenko.

Another picture showed some honey bees pollinating flowers at a nearby lake. These pictures adorned my son's room while he was growing up as a child. One of these years, I hope to meet Valeri and his wife again to thank them for their most generous hospitality, friendship, and water color paintings.

Bees on the Flowers by Valeri Rudenko.

– 9 –
The Hollywood Mystic and Artist

I need to mention one last Russian artist and his wife that I met only briefly near the end of my assignment. The artist Viacheslav Petrov-Gladky had been a member of the Moscow Union of Artists, and some of his works had been published in a catalogue of "Twenty Moscow Artists" in 1981. Since that time, Viacheslav has brought his creative talents to the United States by the name of "Maitreya, The Hollywood Mystic and Artist."

I have not had the opportunity to renew our friendship since we last met in Russia; however, I would describe some of his former art works as very imaginative, spiritual, and mystical. One of his oil paintings entitled "Foggy Distances" was more along the lines of spiritual reality. Viacheslav uses a delicate technique of oil painting that creates an almost three-dimensional picture. The ability to pull the oil outward depicts the painting of a church on a far away hill with fog in the distance and creates a very moving spiritual feeling. His work reveals the passion of a truly creative artist. This painting portrays the hidden talent that serves as a foundation for future discoveries, whether it is in the spiritual world or in the modern world.

Pictures That Inspire Me

Foggy Distances by Viacheslav Petrov-Gladky.

– 10 –
Enduring Strength

A fascinating picture that holds a dear meaning in my life was done by a German exchange student during his visit to Kansas. Martin Falkenberg was one of many exchange students that I have hosted, and he had the opportunity to take a photography course at the Canton-Galva High School as one of his electives. In this novice photography class he took numerous pictures of various sights among the Kansas prairie lands. One notable pic-

Bridge in Kansas by Martin Falkenberg.

ture was that of a stone bridge near Marion, Kansas. The bridge exhibits the enduring strength of an earlier time by its solid construction. As a gift, he presented me this beautiful black and white picture that he photographed and developed as part of his course requirements. He received an "A" for his grade in the class, and I received a treasure of a lifetime. The photographic art will always remind me not only of enduring strength, but of the relationships and respect that others have for our culture and country.

– 11 –
A Birthday Gift

Lastly, I would certainly be remiss by not mentioning the influence that two local Kansas artists from McPherson and Roxbury have had over the many years of my life. Robert Smith of McPherson continues to paint marvelous pictures of our local landscapes, structures, and some European scenes. As a birthday gift from my parents, I was given a painting titled "Shaded Pool." It is a serene picture that emphasizes the calmness and peacefulness along a stream of water. When the mind sees this picture, it is able to relax and reflect on the natural beauty that exists all around us.

Shaded Pool by Robert Smith.

– 12 –
Twin Mounds Lookout

Maleta Forsberg of Roxbury primarily uses the medium of water colors to show the beauty of nature's land, foliage, and animals. This artist has converted a one-room school house into her art gallery adjacent to her country home near Roxbury. She has painted numerous flowers found in Kansas--especially the sunflower, and a variety of birds such as the red-tailed hawk, sparrows, cardinals, geese, pheasants, and mallards. Maleta's artwork shows a true appreciation for the local surroundings of my childhood.

One of her more recent watercolor paintings that I greatly admire is titled "Twin Mounds Lookout." Although most people think of Kansas as only flat lands, we do have a few

Twin Mounds Lookout by Maleta Forsberg.

areas that are above sea level. Twin Mounds happens to be only a few miles from my home in the country near Galva, Kansas. When I was a child, our family would get permission from the landowners. Then we could search the area for arrowheads and climb up and down the mounds. The mounds rise up to 1,539 feet above sea level, and from the top I almost felt that I was on top of the world, especially since I was a small child! The scene as painted by Maleta brings back many fond memories of my childhood, and even today I still enjoy seeing Twin Mounds.

A Range Rider of the Yellowstone

Some day when the last great range herd
    Is held in the valley below,
And the cowboys all have heard the call,
    And know it is time to go;
And the faint dim low of the cattle
    Is heard on the still night air,
And all of the old range-riders
    Seem to be gathering there;
That lone horse and his rider,
    That stands on that great rock wall;
Who knows, but what they have listened
    Until they have heard the call?
And a spirit will stir within them,
    And a smile will cover Bill's face.

He will say, "Come Paint, old partner,
    It is time we took our place."
And the cigarette he is rolling,
    He will light while he's standing there,
Watching his faithful pony
    Snuff the dust-filled air;
Then he'll swing into the saddle,
    As he did in days long past,
And I think he will say, "Old Partner
    This ride will be our last,
For the boys in the valley are calling;
    They are waiting for you and me
To help drive the last great roundup
    Into Eternity."

—Lula A. Cobb

Chapter Two
Inspirational Family Roots

– 13 –
Long Life

It has been my good fortune to have been born in a family that believes in love, respect, honesty, hard work, integrity, perseverance, and faith. My parents were happily married for more than sixty-six years. Unfortunately, my mother, Barbara Louise Cobb, passed away due to a stroke in her middle eighties. My father, Elmon Redell Cobb, has continued to live on the family farm and is presently more than ninety-one years old.

My father's grandmother, Kerstin Olsdotter, was born in the small town of Leksand, Sweden, and immigrated to the United States. She changed her name to Christina Olin when she arrived in America and later married Albert Anderson who came from England and Scotland. Christina Olin came to the state of Kansas because it was open for settlement after the Civil War years.

– 14 –
Swedish, German, and Irish Heritage

My father's mother was Coria Loujency Anderson, one of the daughters of Christina Olin, who was married to Elmon Sickler Cobb. She was a very independent woman and published books and poetry using the name Lula A. Cobb. The Cobb family ancestors originally settled in Pennsylvania and Rhode Island before moving West.

As a child, living in Norway, our family was able to visit Leksand, Sweden, which is very typical of traditional Swedish communities. We were able to trace the Olsdotter name back to the mid-1650's based on the records from the Swedish church located on the shores of Lake Syljon. I was able to visit my father's third cousin, whose home was painted in the traditional red color with white trim around the doors and windows. Most Swedes are very proud of their family history and keep a copy of their family tree in their homes.

My mother's paternal great-grandfather Jacob Holderman lived most of his life in Madison, Kansas. His wife Charlotte Smith Holderman, at the time of her death in 1918, owned more land around Madison than anyone else at that time. After her death the land was divided among several family members and eventually sold. My mother's maternal great-grandfather, Lorenzo Stone, lived in Virgil, Kansas, most of his life. His family heritage can be traced back to Ireland.

Great grandparents John and Clara Holderman.

– 15 –
Walking to Kansas

The oldest relative with whom I could have a genuine conversation was my maternal great-grandmother Clara Lucetta Holderman, who was married to John Holderman, the son of Jacob and Charlotte Holderman. She was able to visit at our home when I was in the first grade and she would teach me to spell some very interesting words, such as pneumonia, hippopotamus, and phthisic.

Phthisic is a disease of the lungs, similar to tuberculosis, and was the cause of death of her husband.

She related to me the story of when she was ten years old and moved from northeastern Missouri to Sumner County in Kansas. She actually walked most of the way beside the two covered wagons drawn by horses. She explained that the family traveled about ten to fifteen miles a day and that the trip took seven weeks. When nightfall came, she and her brothers slept on the ground. On one occasion a bug got in her ear and she felt as if she were going to die. Her mother had to put warm oil in the ear to get the bug out.

– 16 –
The Big Well

When they arrived in Sumner County they lived in a cabin for a few months and then moved on to Kiowa County. There they built a sod house within one week. The floor consisted of dirt and the roof was built with foot-wide boards. The cracks between the boards were covered with smaller strips of wood. A dry creek about a quarter of a mile from the house was where water was obtained by digging a hole two feet deep. They cooked their meals on an old wood-burning stove which had been brought from Missouri. Buffalo chips were used for fuel to heat the stove. Almost every month, she and her father would go to Greensburg to get necessary supplies. Additionally, they got fresh water from the "Big Well," the largest hand-dug well in the world, measuring 109 feet deep and 32 feet in diameter, which has given Greensburg a note of fame. The well was built in 1887 and designed to provide water for the Santa Fe and Rock Island railroads. The twelve-mile trip involved a whole day.

– 17 –
The Great Depression

My mother's parents experienced the Great Depression and believed in being fiscally conservative while working hard. My maternal grandmother Mabel Holderman had a career as a telephone operator for the American Telephone and Telegraph Company, while her husband Earl worked in the oil fields before taking a bookkeeping job with the Kansas Power and Light Company.

– 18 –
Two Brothers and a Sister

My parents came from very diverse European backgrounds. Their heritages complemented their successful marriage. Growing up, I was the second child of four children. My brother Richard was about two years older than I; and, my brother Kinley, about two-years younger. My sister, Reba, was the baby of the family about seven years younger. Since I was the middle boy, I was able to learn from my older brother most of the time. Of course, there was more than enough mischief to go around for everybody. Since my sister was much younger, she had the benefit of three brothers teaching her everything that she needed to know well before her time.

The Cobb Family 1956 – Barbara, Reba, Redell, Richard, Kinley, Marck.

– 19 –
WORLD WAR II AND MILITARY LIFE

My father was a pilot in World War II and flew a variety of fighter aircraft during the war, such as the British Spitfire and the American P-51 Mustang. He was flying 30 miles from Nagasaki, Japan on August 9, 1945, and witnessed the explosion of the atomic bomb dropped by a flight of B-29 bombers.

I was born a few years after the war, and, as a child of a military family, I traveled quite extensively in the United States and Europe. My father spent twenty years serving his country and retired from the Air Force. My mother was always busy as a homemaker, and, later in life, after all of us children became adults, she spent more than sixteen years as an accountant and manager for a large apartment complex in McPherson, Kansas.

During the years that she was performing accounting duties, my father was the manager of the apartment complex. By working together for all of those years, their foresight and attention to detail resulted in the most successfully managed apartment complex which had been subsidized by the federal government. The local Chamber of Commerce designated both of my parents "Honorary" Chamber of Commerce Members because of their success. The apartment complex is now owned by the City of McPherson and remains a success at the time of this writing.

High Flight

Oh, I have slipped the surly bonds of earth
    And danced the skies on laughter-silvered wings;
Sunward I've climbed and joined the tumbling mirth
    Of sun-split clouds—and done a hundred things
You have not dreamed of—wheeled and soared and swung
    High in the sunlit silence. Hovering there,
I've chased the shouting wind along and flung
    My eager craft through footless halls of air.
Up, up the long, delirious, burning blue
    I've topped the wind-swept heights with easy grace,
Where never lark, or even eagle flew;
    And, while with silent, lifting mind I've trod
The high untrespassed sanctity of space,
    Put out my hand, and touched the face of God.

—John Gillespie Magee, Jr.

Chapter Three
Meaningful Sculptures and Symbolism

– 20 –
Graceful Flight at High Altitude

In many ways my hopes and dreams have been symbolized by people, animals, objects, or ideas. Six symbols and sculptures have been an especially meaningful part of my life for several years.

The first of these symbols is the eagle. Not only is it our national symbol, but it is also a personal symbol for me. One of the spectacular characteristics of the eagle is its graceful flight at high altitudes. Since my early years were as a pilot, I can relate to the flight of an eagle.

– 21 –
Eagles and Skydiving

During my summers at the Air Force Academy, I was able to participate in parachute jumping and skydiving. Skydiving was truly an amazing experience because once I began my free fall in the air I could almost fly like an

Bald Eagle by Jules Moigniez

eagle. The serenity and silent beauty of falling through the air made me feel like I could reach out with my hand and touch the face of God. The feeling is the same as expressed by John Gillespie Magee, Jr. in his poem entitled "High Flight."

I was also able to view the eagles flying over the Mississippi River during many of my lunch hours when I worked in Rock Island, Illinois. During the winter time, the eagles would fly over this part of the Mississippi River because the water was not frozen and the location was ideal for the eagles to catch fish. The eagles would fly over the river with their acute visual abilities and use their talons to pluck fish right out of the river. It was truly a spectacular sight to observe.

– 22 –
THE HIGH-RANKING EAGLES

One of my bronze sculptures by the French sculptor Jules Moigniez depicts a large eagle perched upon a branch. The sculpture is a constant reminder of the power and tenacity that are part of the eagle's natural beauty. The proud independence of the eagle represents the strength and freedom that have symbolized our nation. Additionally, the Boy Scouts of America have adopted the eagle as a symbol of its highest rank. Since my son is an Eagle Scout, I am often reminded of his numerous accomplishments to achieve this honor.

I remember the aviator Steve Fossett who set several world aviation records. He, too, was an Eagle Scout. I had the privilege of meeting him when he completed his first solo non-stop round-the-world airplane flight in Salina, Kansas, on March 3, 2005. He flew in an aircraft named the "Virgin Atlantic Global Flyer" and completed his flight in 67 hours, 2 minutes, 38 seconds. Steve was most gracious to have Sir Richard Branson take a photograph of us on that special occasion. When I think of flying and freedom, I think of the natural beauty of the eagle. It will always be a special symbol for me.

Marck and Steve Fossett, 2005.

– 23 –
The Eternal Leaf

My second favorite symbol is a bronze leaf that was sculpted by Imre Varga, Hungary's best known contemporary sculptor. All of my symbols come with a story that makes them personal to me. This particular sculpture was purchased nearly thirteen years ago when Francine and I were on our honeymoon in Budapest, Hungary. This unique bronze leaf sculpture consists of the bronze leaf on a hinge that closes onto an imprint of the leaf in bronze.

What Varga has created is the leaf and its fossilized impression that lasts forever. The name of this piece is "Eternity" which also symbolizes our marriage. When we examined this sculpted leaf, Francine and I both knew that it would be the perfect gift to have as a symbol of our marriage and a memory of our honeymoon.

Eternity by Imre Varga

– 24 –
Building a Civilized World

Since I attended Washburn University School of Law, it was only appropriate to have a small sculpture of the Ichabod, which is the mascot of the school. The Ichabod is a studious-looking student on the run wearing a top-hat and coat-tails, carrying a book. In 1868, the Ichabod Washburn estate bequeathed $25,000 to the university, warranting the changing of the name of the school to Washburn University.

Ichabod Washburn was interested in the moral and intellectual education of students to instill in them the

The Ichabod by Bradbury Thompson.

qualities of independence and happiness. He believed that this training and these qualities would make the students better citizens who would continue to contribute to the building of a civilized world.

The Ichabod mascot and sculpture will always remind me of the quality education that should be made available to all motivated students. Education provides us with the knowledge that is needed to gain an understanding to improve our way of living. In support of my strong belief in the value of education, I have worked to establish three significantly endowed scholarships at three different universities in Kansas to continuously assist outstanding students who desire to pursue higher education at these institutions.

– 25 –
The Unsuccessful Leap

While living on our farm in Galva, our family raised registered polled Hereford cattle and also had a couple of horses. I appreciated the cattle, but the horses seemed to symbolize the intellectual and instinctual qualities that must be understood by humans. Therefore, the horse is another one of my favorite symbols.

On the mantle of our fireplace in our home, my son has a small sculpture of a bronze horse created by Antoine-Louis Barye, who was a 19th Century sculptor of the French Animaliers school. Barye had the incredible ability of capturing the fine details of a horse that allows one to admire the superior qualities of this intelligent animal. Obviously, it is nice to have some "horse sense!"

In Chinese lore, people born in the Year of the Horse are considered popular, cheerful, skillful with money, perceptive, wise, talented, and very independent, although they sometimes talk too much. Both my son and my father were born in the Year of the Horse, so perhaps that is another reason I admire the qualities of the horse.

The horse has long been known for its instinctive traits, able to sense whether a person can be trusted in its presence. I am sure there are other animals that also have these very instinctive traits, but the horse is special due to its size and because it can be dangerous to those who are not will-

Thoroughbred Horse by Antoine-Louis Barye.

ing to be understanding. On most occasions, I have found horses to be friendly, and they have found me to be friendly.

However, on one occasion, I was riding a young thoroughbred, and, when I attempted to make a small jump, the horse made a couple of roundabout motions and then threw me to the ground. After about the third unsuccessful attempt, I decided that the independent thoroughbred could have its way, and the horse and I enjoyed the remainder of the time galloping across the fields. Perhaps, if I had had a little more horse sense, I could have understood why this thoroughbred did not want to make a small leap!

– 26 –
To Speak the Truth

The Indian chief has long been one of my favorite symbols, representing leadership and the Great Spirit Chief. Carl Kauba, an Austrian sculptor, had a great affection for the Indians of the American West and created many sculptures depicting the American West. His sculpture of Chief Joseph on horseback is another one of my favorite sculptures to admire. Chief Joseph is shown wearing a very detailed headdress while sitting with great pride on his horse. He was a true leader, and his quotes remain part of his living legacy.

Chief Joseph stated, "All men were made by the Great Spirit Chief. They are all brothers." He also said, "It does not require many words to speak the truth." These simple statements are the marks of a great leader. In the early

1800's Chief Joseph's tribe had good relations with the whites after the Lewis and Clark expedition. However, several years later, following the gold rush to the Northwest Territory, his tribe was forced onto reservations. For several years he resisted the government but eventually surrendered with a speech that immortalized him as a military leader in American popular culture.

Chief Joseph on Horseback by Carl Kauba.

– 27 –
Political Correctness

Another reason I admire the Indian chief is the fact that, while attending high school in Galva, our school mascot was the chieftain. However, due to political correctness, the mascot was changed to an eagle. I enjoy both the eagle and the chief. Both sculptures have special meanings that express pride and freedom. These are attributes that give my life contentment.

– 28 –
Balancing Life

The last sculpture with symbolism is entitled "The Idle Fiddle" by Leon Tharel. It shows a young boy sleeping with the fiddle supported by his shoulder. The fiddler depicted was theoretically Mozart as a child. This piece of art relates to the creative talents that are associated with music. It is especially meaningful because, when my son was a very young age he was playing the violin. Today he writes music, sings, and plays the bass guitar and the acoustic guitar. The sculpture speaks to maintaining a balance in life while taking time out to rest.

No doubt, I appreciate the ability to relax, and admire the ability to play musical instruments. There is nothing wrong with hard work, but we must also take time out to smell the roses and enjoy the talents that one has been given. "The Idle Fiddle" provides a sense of balance in our

The Idle Fiddle by Leon Tharel.

daily lives and the realization that sleep is important. It also illustrates the importance of enjoying musical talents by observing and listening.

– 29 –
Knowledge and Understanding

Although material objects such as sculptures and pictures can inspire and enhance the meaning of our personal lives, they are not, by any measure, absolute necessities. What gives our lives true meaning is the knowledge and understanding of what one acquires through education and experience. Our families, friends,

Meaningful Sculptures and Symbolism

and communities all contribute to this important meaning, which makes each one of us unique individuals. It is this environment that gives our lives value and the ability to help others while recognizing that life is a continual learning process for everyone in our small world.

Our Kansas
Ad Astra Per Aspera

Where North meets South and East meets West,
There lies the state that we love best;
With motto flung across the sky,
Our faith and courage cannot die.
Out where the wheat fields gleam like gold,
Out where a million blessings fold
Our hearts in peace and sweet content—
That's Kansas—the magnificent.

Where North meets South and East meets West,
There lies the state that we love best;
Where sunflowers toss a golden sea,
Where meadowlarks trill a melody;
Where cottonwoods in stateliness
Bespeak our native friendliness.
Stars write our motto through the skies;
Beneath it courage never dies.

—Ovie Pedigo Tanner

Chapter Four
Pillars of My Spiritual Foundation

– 30 –
Withstanding Challenges

What have been the pillars in my life that have enabled me to achieve a life of contentment? First, and perhaps foremost, is a high degree of faith and spirituality that has given me the strength to withstand the numerous challenges and hardships that have presented themselves along this lengthy pathway. Some of these challenges were instigated by me; others were simply thrown at me.

The first of these challenges was simply to get an education. I can remember my first grade class at Thomas Jefferson Elementary School in Wichita, Kansas, where my learning initially began. I had a nice class, but my teacher, Mrs. Warner, just seemed to be too strict and in my young opinion, not very compassionate. But my parents reinforced the learning process, and with the faith that hard work and continued persistence would payoff, I managed to pass the first grade. That first year in school was the most significant because it taught me the importance of being focused in my life. It was one of the first pillars to be set in the building of my foundation.

– 31 –
Trust and Understanding

Another example of my faith and spirituality can be found in two of my favorite Biblical scriptures. The first is found in Proverbs 3: 5-6 which says, "Trust in the Lord with all your heart and lean not unto your own understanding. Acknowledge Him in all your ways and He will direct your path." The second is found in Philippians 4:13 which states, "I can do all things through Christ who strengthens me." These two passages to me are the essence of faith and spirituality. My Uncle Clayton said that these were his favorite verses in the Bible and after many decades, I concur with his view. It is necessary to have the strength of such wise words to keep us moving forward in the right direction. My faith and spirituality help me to understand that there is a God and that God is love. It is my belief that God has given us a purpose wherever we are born and wherever we are living in this world.

– 32 –
Freedom Is Not Free

I was blessed to be born in the United States and to have lived most of my life in the state of Kansas. The life values learned in Kansas created a second pillar of my foundation that encouraged me to pursue my formal education. Indeed, from the quality of learning I received, I feel a sense of indebtedness to give something back to our country, state, and community where I was raised and educated.

One of the reasons that I served twenty years with the United States Air Force was because I wanted to protect, defend, and preserve the values of our country. We have

Air Force Retirement 1990 – Lt. Col. Marck Cobb and parents, Barbara and Redell.

all learned through our history that freedom is not free. In our short history as a country, too many lives have been sacrificed to maintain our freedom, our security, and our ideals. I have lost several friends who fought in the Southeast Asia Conflict. I consider myself very fortunate to have survived twenty years of service to our country.

– 33 –
Win-Win Solutions

I am proud of those twenty years and would gladly make the same decision again to preserve our way of life. Since retiring from the Air Force, I spent another twenty years as an attorney at law, licensed in the State of Kansas. During my legal career I lived in Colorado, Illinois, and Kansas. The experience in the legal profession taught me that it is possible to achieve "win-win" solutions. I worked as the General Counsel for an insurance organization to solve problems, and later I worked as a legal mediator in Kansas for ten years.

– 34 –
Bonus for Paying Attention

I taught business law at Western Illinois University in Moline, Illinois, for one year. During that time, one of my female students approached me after class and said she wanted to thank me for teaching the course. She explained that she had applied one of the lessons that I had taught on equal employment and opportunity. She had used this information in a discussion with her employer and had received a significant increase in salary that was comparable to what her male co-workers were making. It was most gratifying to hear that my students were actually paying attention and applying what they had learned. I felt honored to have made a difference in at least one person's life.

– 35 –
One Big, Diverse Family

The final pillars of my foundation have been community and family. Since I spent my high school years in a town of about 300 people, everyone knew everybody, and, in many ways, the community and family were really just one big, diverse family. During my high school years, it seemed as though everyone was a participant in church, plays, sports, or work that continuously kept us in social contact with one another.

For example, I sang in the church choir; acted in the school plays; and, participated in football, basketball, and track. During the summers, I worked on the farm plowing the fields and bailing hay. I was also employed at the local grain elevator in town during the wheat harvest and worked many long hours.

These family and community activities have continued throughout my life. They have provided many friendships for growth, development, and understanding. Presently, or in the recent past, I have served on the Galva Christian

Church Board, the McPherson Museum and Arts Foundation Board, the local American Red Cross Board, and the Board of Governors for the Washburn Law School Alumni Association. Each of these areas represents my core beliefs: specifically, a concern for spiritual values; respect for the past, present, and future; an interest in community health care; and, a concern for education.

Spiritual values come from faith, church, and God. A respect for the past, present, and future is a commitment and understanding of our country, state, and family. The value of community health care is an important part of any community and family. Lastly, we must continue our education if we are going to prosper and hopefully leave this world a better place for future generations to live in than when we entered it.

*"Man's flight through life is sustained
by the power of his knowledge."*

—Austin "Dusty" Miller

Chapter Five
Teachers of Wisdom

– 36 –
Get to Work

In my life I have spent more than twenty years getting some kind of formal education, culminating in my law degree. Interestingly, a law degree is considered a terminal degree. According to academia, a terminal degree is the highest professional degree in a particular field of study. In my humble opinion, after that much education, one had better start getting some hands-on experience. One should take a break from the continuous pursuit of an academic education that has never been put into practice. Perhaps "terminal" simply means to stop the educational process and get to work!

– 37 –
A Time and Place for Reflection

During this educational process, I was extremely fortunate to have numerous outstanding, compassionate, understanding, and giving teachers and professors. Although most of my instructors were, in fact, humans, one of my favorite teachers simply came from nature. I would definitely consider nature an important teacher during my educational process.

As a young child around the age of seven, I managed to find a piece of unwanted wood that had perhaps been part of a wooden hay trailer. The flat piece of wood was about three by four feet and, for me, it was very heavy. As a small, innocent lad, I had to be very creative to find a way to move it nearly half a mile to my favorite tree in a small grove area. I am not sure, but it probably took me a whole day to move that piece of wood.

The next trick was to get that piece of wood up into the tree on a large branch that was about eight feet above the ground. With lots of desire and persistence, I accomplished the challenge. I used some large nails to provide foot-holds on the tree trunk so that I could climb up that eight-foot height. Then, being very efficient, I managed to use some more of the large nails to attach the wooden platform to the large forked tree branch. I spent many hours lying on that wooden platform receiving lessons from one of my earliest teachers. That teacher was the Kansas wind and blue summer sky.

My open air tree platform allowed me a time and place for reflection on nature. Now I believe it was an early form of meditation. Later in my life, I would show my young son Layton that same branch. I would help him climb to that big branch, and I would stand below him while he jumped for a two-foot free fall until I caught him in my arms. It follows, like father, like son—we both experienced a thrill climbing and playing on that tree!

If my parents or "big daddy" government had been around in those days, I am sure that my actions as a young child and later as a father might have been considered a form of child endangerment. I thought of it as behaving like Tom Sawyer and Huckleberry Finn--a real life adventure and a learning experience. For me, the Kansas wind and summer sky allowed me to think freely and focus as well as dream. It helped develop my spiritual faith. I con-

Layton on the tree branch.

tinue to have a high regard and deep appreciation for the natural wonders of our state and the world. This is where part of my optimistic motivation and passion comes from--the free spirit of the wind, one of my very first teachers.

– 38 –
The Norwegian Experience

The next teacher that definitely had an impact on my life was Mr. Osterman. He was my sixth-grade teacher in the Oslo American School in Oslo, Norway. To this day, I still attend reunions with my sixth-grade classmates from Oslo. I was attending school in Norway because my father was working as an executive officer for the North Atlantic Treaty Organization (NATO) that had headquarters in Oslo. This was my dad's last military assignment, and it would be the last time that I would attend a school in a foreign country as a child.

– 39 –
Captain John Smith

Mr. Osterman was an outstanding teacher and taught all of my classes in the sixth grade for my second semester. My first semester of the sixth grade had been in England. I attended the same school that Captain John Smith had attended during the Pocahontas and John Smith days in the early 1600's. The more than 450-year-old school was the King Edward VI Grammar School located in the town of Louth. At that school, there was a separate teacher for every subject. Going back to one teacher for all of my subjects in the second semester in Oslo was much easier for me.

– 40 –
The Backward R

The one idea that I remember the most was when Mr. Osterman taught geography class. He drew a backward R on the blackboard and asked the class what it represented. Of course, no one knew. He explained that it was the Russian alphabetical letter pronounced "ya." That tiny piece of information stayed with me through all of my life. Ever since that day, I wanted to know more about a country that used letters that were backwards from ours. That tiny seed eventually grew to learning the Russian language. Later, on two separate occasions, I was a representative from the United States to Russia.

– 41 –
Meeting President Gorbachev

The first occasion was in 1980 when I served for two years in Moscow as an Assistant Air Force Attaché. The second occasion was in 1990 when I was part of a United States government-sponsored lawyer exchange program to meet Soviet lawyers in Moscow in the Kremlin for a week-long seminar about the rule of law. On that

Bob Wise, President Gorbachev and Marck, Lindsborg, Kansas, 2005.

occasion I had the opportunity to personally meet President Mikhail Gorbachev.

Fifteen years later, I again met President Gorbachev in Lindsborg, Kansas, when he visited the Karpov Chess School in Lindsborg. The world we live in is small. Mr. Osterman provided the motivation for me to learn more and to succeed in the opportunity to work with and listen first-hand to our number one Cold War adversary: the Soviet Union. So, teachers, keep up the good work because you never know what your students will do with the information you provide in the classroom!

– 42 –
THE VOLUNTEER SPIRIT

One of my high school teachers, Velma Williams, demonstrated the power of all kinds of speaking methods, such as speaking for entertainment, extemporaneously, persuasively, or for a dramatic presentation. She encouraged me to pursue forensic competitions. She was extremely creative and knew how to express her views in a passionate and meaningful manner. She was my forensics coach, and her confidence in me motivated me to compete in extemporaneous and dramatic presentations that resulted in outstanding awards at state competitions. This was an extracurricular activity, but she devoted much of her out-of classroom time to help all students in forensic activities.

We have some outstanding teachers that are fully dedicated to see students excel outside of the classroom, but not nearly enough. I believe that truly outstanding teachers are willing to take on extracurricular activities to broaden a student's academic learning. Their ultimate reward is watching the students succeed from these experiences. Unfortunately, my old high school today no longer exists, and the new high school does not offer this particular kind of extracurricular activity. However, Velma Williams' spirit is what encouraged me to serve as a volunteer coach for ten years to assist students who wanted to participate in the extracurricular activity of chess. All of us need to find and spend more time teaching and helping our students in activities that have life-long values.

– 43 –
Looking for the King

While I was attending both elementary and high school, I met a fourth-grade teacher who truly inspired me as well as her fourth-grade students. Her name was Donna Hamilton. She knew how to make learning fun and exciting. I will always be indebted to her for the influence she had on my academic years in Galva. Even though she was never my classroom teacher, she would make herself available to assist me whenever I needed a critique on a speaking presentation.

Donna Hamilton eventually became a family friend and attended my university graduation from the United States Air Force Academy. During that occasion, she experienced an interesting problem with her lodging accommodations. My parents had made the reservations at the same hotel and, of course, they were interested in how "Aunt" Donna liked her room. She stated, "When I entered my room, I saw this beautiful king bed, but there was a problem. I looked all around the room and under the bed but could not find any king!" She had a great sense of humor that inspired us to live life with laughter, and we always enjoyed her friendship.

– 44 –
Heart-felt Giving

Let me provide an illustration about the connectivity between teachers and people in general. My eighth-grade primary teacher was Don Margreiter, and he was always willing to listen and help students become better. He was responsible for introducing me to Donna Hamilton. Don Margreiter also had a daughter who became a fifth-grade teacher, Sue Unruh. Both Sue Unruh and Donna Hamilton have been able to inspire their students and have the ability to make learning fun.

Sue Unruh, was my son's fifth-grade teacher. I think a part of my son's success can be attributed to her influential character. She continues to be one of the most outstanding elementary teachers at the Canton-Galva Middle School. Both Sue and Donna epitomize the true, heart-felt giving that superior teachers share with their students. These are the kind of teachers that we would all want our children to have in the classroom.

– 45 –
A Unique Learning Experience

Two professors during my Master's Degree studies at the Naval Postgraduate School in Monterey, California, deserve recognition. They are Kurt London and Claude Buss. Kurt London was my Soviet Foreign Policy professor. That particular class was a one-on-one instruction that required me to read one book a week on Soviet foreign policy and then spend a couple of hours discussing the issues with him. It was a very unique learning experience, and one that I will always cherish. I was fortunate that he took me as a student. He also introduced me to many of his academic friends and colleagues in Monterey and Washington, D.C. These extracurricular events greatly enriched the learning process and acknowledged the mutual respect that existed between the professor and his student.

Claude Buss taught me Soviet and Chinese Relations and History. He was extraordinary in that he took two of us from his classroom in Monterey to meet with his friends and colleagues in Washington, D.C. The intellectual exchanges and experiences prepared me well for my future endeavors, especially as an attaché in the Soviet Union.

– 46 –
The Thinking Process

In my law school years at the University of Washburn School of Law in Topeka, Kansas, I had several top-notch professors, but I was especially impressed with Jim Concannon. He taught first-year students a course in Civil Procedure. What made his class somewhat unusual was that he not only taught the knowledge of the law, but he also taught the purpose and ideas behind the law. He always did his best to make us understand the many different perspectives that must be taken into account when analyzing and making a legal decision or in creating a new precedent. His thinking process and method of teaching instilled in me the diligent and deliberative thought process that goes into making good decisions throughout our lives. Jim Concannon later became one of the most successful deans in the history of the Washburn University School of Law.

– 47 –
Leadership by Example

When I reminisce about the many teachers in my life, I must consider myself extremely blessed to have had the good fortune of so many wonderful teachers that gave so much of themselves to their students. Teachers play a major role in the development of our youth and their impact for future generations. Their job is certainly one that must include leadership by example. It is my personal goal to provide and instill in others that important value of leadership by example.

Guiding Star

Feeling lonely, feeling bad;
Feeling empty, feeling sad.

Living day, and leaving world;
You were stronger in this world.

Only love could save your life;
Love is what you dreamt about.

And you met the one you saw
In your dreams, fell in love with her.

Feeling thankful, knowing that
If not for her, you would fall apart.

Worshiping her day and night;
Thanking God for living life.

Shining like a guiding star;
Love brings sense to our lives.

—Artem Kononov

Chapter Six
The School of Hard-Knocks

– 48 –
COMPASSION AND FORGIVENESS

As we all know, none of us are perfect. I have learned that our imperfections help us to become more compassionate and forgiving. In more than sixty years of life, I have been married for about twenty-five years. For more than half of those years I have been married to Francine. She has always been loving, understanding, and supportive in both good times and hard times. I feel that this is probably true in any successful and happy marriage.

– 49 –
LOVE WINS

Francine and I were introduced by a mutual friend at a meeting in Washington, D.C., in 1995. At first, I was hesitant to get involved, having had two previous faulty relationships. However, love won out. Francine proved to be much too irresistible. In March of 1997, I stopped at the Court House in Goodland, Kansas, and obtained a marriage license. Then, at a small family ceremony in my parents' country home we were married on March 21st. The following May we celebrated our marriage with a church wedding. Since then, we have continued to work and find time for each other while helping to care for both of our parents.

Marck and Francine.

– 50 –
THE TRUE MEANING OF LOVE

During our courtship, on one occasion Francine borrowed my car to visit a client about 30 miles from where we were vacationing in the mountains in Colorado. When she was returning from her business, the snow began falling on the mountain roads, and the Interstate became rather dangerous. The unexpected accident occurred when a large semi-truck collided with her car, causing damage on all sides of the car. Of course, the only immediate thought I had was for her safety. Suffice it to say, the value of the car is absolutely nothing when compared to the value of the person. I think these are some of the tests that committed people face, and such an experience allows them to grow closer together as they realize how short life can be. They recognize the true meaning of love and compassion.

As I mentioned earlier, before I met and married Francine, I had been previously married. I do not think one can be proud of an unsuccessful relationship, but hopefully one can learn from the past and find someone in the future who will mutually share compassion, understanding, support, and love. I have found these attributes in Francine, but they were only discovered after traveling down the road of hard knocks. For this reason, I will share a couple of my more imperfect relationships and the lessons learned.

– 51 –
Substituting Independence for Marriage

My first marriage was to a woman who was talented, supporting, and wanted to have a family as I did. Unfortunately, with all due respect, she lived in a state of fear created unintentionally by her mother and grandmother. Her father had died when she was very young, and she had been raised by her mother and grandmother living under the same roof. One of the fears instilled by these women was a high degree of pain associated with childbirth. I think this hidden fear only became worse the longer we were married and I was unable to alleviate such fear successfully.

She continued her education to eventually become a lawyer. I think she was willing to substitute independence for marriage. I feel that this was the major reason for going our separate ways. We departed in peace, but she demanded a lot from our eight years of marriage. I still wish her happiness in her chosen way of life.

– 52 –
If It Is Too Good to Be True

The second marriage was very different. I was totally infatuated and convinced that we would live together forever. During the six months of dating she was the most bubbly, happy, loving, energetic, and supportive woman I had ever met. Any disagreements we had appeared to be resolvable. Shortly after our marriage, we were blessed with a son who only brought more joy to our lives. However, if it is too good to be true, then it probably is.

Somehow the love and happiness turned into depression and destructiveness. No amount of counseling could change the situation when my son was about six months old. We had sessions with two different marital counselors, and she refused to continue counseling. The situation only became worse. Neither my actions nor my words, as a husband or friend, could improve our situation.

– 53 –
Substituting the Soap Opera for Marriage

Two years later we officially divorced in a soap-opera fashion. The lawyers received lots of money for many years. The post-divorce soap opera continued until my son graduated from high school. As much as I wanted my second marriage to succeed, it did not. I realize it takes two and that there must be a happy medium, but I did not want to go through another break-up. I thought I would never love and marry again. It was a difficult lesson to learn, and just as difficult to recover from this kind of relationship.

– 54 –
Faith and Trust in God

Fortunately, God works in mysterious ways. Five years later I met and married Francine. We have been blessed with a peaceful, loving, and understanding relationship that has lasted for nearly thirteen years. Francine believes in integrity, hard work, and mutual respect for others. She has always provided unconditional love and support in our marriage. Certainly, our life has been challenged with work demands and family, but we have faith and trust in God that our life together will continue to be a loving, happy and rewarding experience.

– 55 –
Appearances Can Be Deceiving

Another story in my life happened about 25 years ago when I was assigned as a flight instructor for air refueling operations at McConnell Air Force Base in Wichita, Kansas. It taught me the very important and expensive lesson that appearances can be extremely deceiving. Additionally, it taught me that government-run bureaucracies do not like to admit mistakes even after the truth is shown and proven. This experience taught me that pearls are born out of irritation. Personally, I would like to think pearls could be made some other way!

On a beautiful summer, blue-sky day, I was asked to provide flight instruction for an aircrew on a Saturday morning flight. Since I was dedicated to my job, I agreed to volunteer for the extra duty that weekend. I was given less than 24 hours' notice, and I had absolutely no input in developing the plan of flight. About an hour before the flight was scheduled to depart, I was informed of the flight plan and that the air refueling location would be in the airspace near my parents' farm. Therefore, I made a call to my parents and told them that they could probably view our flight if they wanted to look for it in the clear skies nearby where they lived. This decision would later prove to be problematic.

After the air refueling and after some training for the navigator, our flight was returning to land at the air base. At that point in time, I was the pilot in command and

Major Cobb, far right, with his regular air crew.

was instructing the new co-pilot on the aircrew how to plan an enroute descent. All of this information had been coordinated with the air traffic controller, and our flight was continuously under radar control based on our instrument flight rules.

However, during the descent, the non-instructor pilot, who was not flying the aircraft and who had not been following the activities of the flight, came into the cockpit to observe our enroute descent. Then, without any consultation with either pilot, he somehow determined in his mind, based on the appearance of my instruction, that we were not flying in accordance with the instrument flight rules.

At this point, he unilaterally determined that we were flying under visual flight rules. This would have meant that we would not be under radar control and we would not be required to fly by instrument flight rules. This could only have occurred if a request had been formally made to the air traffic controllers, and no such request had ever been made. This distinction about flight rules is key to the rest of the story created by the pilot who was partially observing and was not flying the aircraft.

– 56 –
The Creation of a False Story

By making the false claim that we were flying under visual flight rules, he then claimed that we were flying only at an altitude of 500 feet above ground level as opposed to the minimum requirement of 1,000 feet above the ground mandated for instrument flight rules. The final claim created by the non-flying pilot was that I was personally flying over my parents' farm at 500 feet above the ground illegally. In flying jargon, this is called "buzzing" a particular location. I was neither flying over the farm of my parents nor was I flying at an altitude of 500 feet. Admittedly, I was within a few miles of where my parents lived, and it would be possible to see our aircraft at the higher altitude that we were flying.

Sometime within the next twenty-four hours after the flight, this non-flying pilot told his fictional story to his flight commander who was in line to be the next squadron commander. The present squadron commander had personally recommended that this individual be his replacement. Then, without any substantiation of the non-flying pilot's story, my boss, the squadron commander, proceeded to inform the hierarchy in the bureaucracy that he had a problem with my flying instruction.

Forty-eight hours later, I was called in by my boss and was informed that I was guilty of being a hooligan in the air. I simply told my boss that the events he had described to me were totally wrong. Furthermore, I explained the events to him and informed him that I could prove every detail of my story to be fully accurate based on the tapes of the air traffic controllers who directed, approved, and monitored our flight. If there had been a problem with the flight, the air traffic controllers would have immediately issued an air traffic control violation, or at a minimum, they would have notified my boss for not complying with the instrument flight rules.

–57–
Trumping Up the Charges

The only problem with the truth of my story was that my boss asked for the information after making a fateful decision based on the fictional story. Rather than admit his mistake to his superiors, my boss convinced his superiors that he would act based on the false story. I can only imagine that he thought that he would keep his record clean and, since I worked for him and was the low man on the totem pole, I would go along. Needless to say, my boss failed to understand that he was attacking my honesty and integrity.

I refused to accept a letter of reprimand that was recommended by my boss. That meant that my boss and the bureaucracy had to decide to either back down or convene a formal court-martial. Unfortunately for me, the decision was made to create more trumped up charges and to convene a court-martial. Eventually, after six months, the bureaucracy was able to force a court-martial. During the trial, the air traffic control tapes proved every detail of my story to be true. The fictional story was also proven to have no truthful merits. Twenty minutes after closing arguments, I was fully acquitted. However, the bureaucracy still continued the fight and stated in writing that I was guilty.

– 58 –
Guilty Until Proven Innocent

Subsequently, I was reassigned about six months later to a very rewarding assignment at the Air University in Montgomery, Alabama, as a research analyst. Since the bureaucracy at McConnell Air Force Base had declared me to be guilty in writing, it prevented me from being promoted. Thus, after one year in my new job, I was faced with doing my duties with no opportunity of a promotion or to do something better with my life.

I decided to resign from the Air Force after sixteen years of service and received no benefits. I spent the next few years attending law school in Topeka, Kansas, while the bureaucracy slowly reviewed my case based on administrative procedures. Within four months of entering classes at law school, I began working in one of the divisions of the Office of the Attorney General of Kansas. A few months later I began an additional job working in bankruptcy law and a third job working with regulations for the state legislature. I spent my final few months in law school attending classes and working in two legal positions to pay my way through law school.

– 59 –
The Bureaucracy Gets It Right

After five years of reviewing my case against the Air Force, the Secretary of the Air Force finally overturned the mistakes that had been made against me and reinstated me with all benefits. I returned to work for the Air Force in a very prestigious assignment at the Pentagon.

Although I did not truly enjoy the experience of being charged with a felonious offense, I can honestly state that the experience solidified my desire and passion to do what is right. I paid a high price to do what was right, but in a lifetime of more than sixty years, I have absolutely no regrets. In the end, the tragic experience made me a better and more compassionate and understanding person. I received my promotions, and all the other parties, including my former boss and a few generals, did not receive any promotions. Given enough time and effort, the bureaucracy can get it right!

There have been other lessons that I have learned in life, but my previous marriages and false accusations by the Air Force bureaucracy are definitely the most significant events that got my full attention. I do not have any regrets and I forgive those who have made false statements about me. These lessons are character-building, but I would not recommend these methods or experiences as ways to learn to have a stronger character. The school of hard knocks is never easy, but having the perseverance and desire to reach your goals is worth the effort.

Bits and Pieces

I believe in God's master plan in lives. He moves people in and out of each others lives and each leaves his mark on the other. You find you are made of bits and pieces of all who have touched your life, and you are more because of it, and would be less if they had not touched you.

Pray God that you can accept the bits and pieces in humility and wonder, and never question, and never regret.

Chapter Seven
Influential Friendships

– 60 –
The Research Project

When I was completing my university studies, one of my psychology courses required me to do a research project on the characteristics that people attribute to their best friends. Many descriptions were written about attributes of a best friend, but one of the most often used phrases was "a person who would give you the shirt off his back." Other popular descriptions were "a person who could be trusted" and "one who would be with you in time of need." I have found these descriptions to be true of the characteristics of people that have had the greatest influence and impact on my life. My story would be incomplete if I did not briefly mention a few of these friends and some of the reasons that they have remained life-long friends.

– 61 –
Picking Oranges in Phoenix

I believe that two of my most compassionate friends, whom I have known for more than forty years, would have to include Jack and Gladys Bobo from Phoenix, Arizona. I first met Jack and Gladys when I was participating in a choral group from my university that was giving a performance in Phoenix. Jack and Gladys assisted in hosting and accommodating a couple of the members of our group. Fortunately, I was one of the members who was assigned to them. During that occasion, I learned the importance of giving and sharing your personal time and life.

It was the first time in my life that I had been in Phoenix and could walk into the backyard and pick oranges for breakfast in the month of January. The most generous hospitality that we received from the Bobo family left a genuine realization of the kind-heartedness and sincere feelings that exist among our vast population. Throughout the years since that first visit, I have had the opportunity and pleasure to share the beliefs and common-sense attitudes that have been the basis for their success and happiness.

– 62 –
Invitation to Dinner

The next couple I met also became life-long friends of mine; however, the events that led to our meeting occurred under a very different set of circumstances. I was defending my honesty and integrity in my Air Force career due to false accusations that I have detailed in the previous chapter. I had been given a recommendation to contact a retired Air Force colonel who was familiar with problems associated with biased accusations made by overzealous commanders in the Air Force.

At the time, I was attending law school, and I had a few days during a semester break which I used to make a personal visit to deliver my complex administrative appeal. This involved traveling from Kansas to Virginia to make a "special delivery" of the background material that was needed to write the administrative appeal. Colonel Clement Counts and his wife Terry greeted me at door of their home when I arrived. It was then that Terry showed a totally unexpected gesture of compassion by inviting me to stay for dinner.

This simple act of generosity and compassion communicated a mutual trust and friendship that has endured ever since that first meeting. The wisdom and advice that Clem and Terry have given to me over the many years of our friendship has demonstrated the power that a few acts of kindness and generosity can do. Their compassion is greatly beneficial for helping others to overcome their challenges.

– 63 –
Sharing Common Values

One of the most important qualities of friendship is trust and understanding. Jim and Becky Wiederstein, who live in Colorado, have been friends of mine since we attended high school in Kansas. The ability to share family values and experiences with friends provides support and confidence that is reassuring when raising a family. The numerous stories that concern children and other relatives can be shared in a trusted manner with those friends whom you have known most of your life.

I am sure that most people have this kind of friendship. It is important that we recognize the value of these relationships. All too often these vital relationships are taken for granted or, in some instances, the relationship is allowed to evaporate. I want to emphasize the significance of having trustworthy friends who are willing to be understanding and available during the good and difficult situations that we face at one time or another.

– 64 –
The Match-Makers

Throughout our lives we continue to discover new friends as we continue to interact with people and grow older. A perfect example is the couple that introduced me to my wife. I had known Cotton (his nickname) and Jonni Finch as acquaintances while I was working as general counsel for an insurance organization. Fortunately, after several years, Jonni decided to play match-maker and arranged to have me meet Francine. Since then, we have all become the best of friends.

Jonni is a friend who is always open to new ideas and willing to think outside the box. She is very confident and full of hope and faith in people who do good things to improve the lives of others. Her husband Cotton brings a wealth of wisdom and philosophy to our friendship. We continue to spend time together, expressing our thoughts and feelings about helping others and seeking self-improvement as well.

– 65 –
THE DANISH CONNECTION

All of these relationships exemplify all of the best qualities of friendship, but understanding the highlights of each friend is what brought us together initially. The last couple illustrates the joy of international friendships. Ole and Britta Nielsen are Danes whom I met when I was attending pilot training in Oklahoma forty years ago. Ole was one of the Danish exchange pilots in our training group. Of course, the Danes were new to the American culture, but we all had a mutual respect for each other and the different cultures that we came from. Following our pilot training, we have been able to successfully maintain our friendship over the years.

The qualities that standout with Ole and Britta are their ability to adapt to different living conditions and their creativity. Ole flew for the Danish Air Force and then became a pilot for the Scandinavian Airlines System. His wife Britta has been a creative photographer. We all enjoy the people and cultural relationships that give our lives added meaning and a quality of life that cannot be duplicated.

I hope that these qualities of friendship will inspire others to look for such characteristics in their new and old friends. People who have compassion, trust, faith, respect, creativeness, confidence, wisdom, charity, and hospitality are those special friends that one will cherish forever.

What God Hath Promised

God hath not promised skies always blue
Flower-strewn pathways all our lives through;
God hath not promised sun without rain,
Joy without sorrow, peace without pain.

But God hath promised strength for the day,
Rest for the labor, light for the way,
Grace for the trials, help from above,
Unfailing sympathy, undying love.

—Annie Johnson Flint

Chapter Eight
Simple Beliefs

– 66 –
BORN WITH GOODNESS

My general philosophy has always been very basic. It is simply do the right thing the best way possible. I am thankful that everyone in this world is a little bit different from everyone else. These differences are to be appreciated, respected, and used in constructive ways. Every one of us is born with goodness. We just have to recognize it and use it.

– 67 –
ANALYZE AND LISTEN

Sometimes I refer to my philosophy by the acronym "KISS," which stands for "Keep It Simple Stupid." All too often we analyze simple problems and develop some very complex solutions. A perfect example of this is the 2,000-page health care bill that has been produced by our

Congress and submitted to the legislature for a vote in 2010. I have discovered that most of our daily life problems can be resolved with much simpler solutions. Certainly, major problems should seek solutions that will not create more significant problems for future generations.

In my legal mediation practice I facilitated many solutions. These were accomplished by listening carefully to both sides of a position and crafting a solution that was both reasonable and practical. This was especially important when dealing with marital problems and divorce cases.

On one occasion a mother would not agree to any proposed solutions, many of which were very reasonable. After a few more counseling sessions, the obstacle that prevented any agreement was found to be a loving parent who had told his daughter to never agree on the issue that was being discussed and needed mediation. When we were able to confront the obstacle and determine that there was no basis for the obstruction, then a fair and reasonable agreement was accomplished that satisfied all parties.

Had we not been careful listeners or had we not been patient, we would still be at a point of no agreement. This creates non-productive living arrangements and leaves no one happy or satisfied. If I want change, I must first start within myself. My philosophy has been one of perseverance and heart-felt desire to do what is right. Hopefully this view is able to find the facts and get close to the real truth of the issues that are creating problems. My belief is that if we look for the facts and search for the truth, then we have a greatly enhanced chance of solving our problems in a rational manner.

– 68 –
ACHIEVING SUCCESS AND HAPPINESS

A few years ago I read a book called "The Four Agreements" by Miguel Ruiz, a former medical doctor and surgeon who is now writing about philosophy. His book is based on ancient Toltec wisdom, which describes a way of life based on the esoteric Toltec knowledge that was passed on through many generations. Although it is not a religion, the Toltec wisdom embraces the human spirit.

His book is based on the belief that subscribes to four agreements that will enable us as individuals to achieve success and happiness in life. These four agreements serve as outstanding goals that one should try to achieve. Many times, when I hear people who are arguing or people who are distressed, I suggest they attempt to follow and understand these four agreements because they are concise, simple, and easy to remember.

The first agreement is "Be impeccable with your word." Not surprisingly, more stress and arguments are caused by misunderstandings. These misunderstandings can usually be traced to the way something was said by words or intonation or, in some cases, what was not said. If you are not impeccable with your word, then, whenever the meaning is not clear, you will probably be subjected to Murphy's Law: "If something can go wrong, it will." It definitely helps to have someone else reflect on our statements, and then we will have a better ability to determine if that reflection is indeed the meaning we were intended.

We do not live in a perfect world! In today's environment of political correctness and change, statements made by one generation can be totally misunderstood by another generation. All too often arguments are created from statements taken out of context without any consideration of answering the important questions of who, what, when, where, and why. Sometimes we need to thoroughly digest a statement to fully understand its meaning and application. A little more patience and understanding would alleviate many arguments.

The second agreement is "Do not make any assumptions." How many times during the routine course of events during any one day do we make assumptions? I think we probably make more than a million assumptions daily, but, if we tried to limit a small percentage of them, one would most likely be much happier and would be living a less stressful and more productive life.

Of course, the only sure way not to make an assumption is for all individuals to be impeccable with their words. That is not going to happen anytime soon, but at least we can learn to recognize and be aware of the fact that, if we are dealing with an assumption, we might have the opportunity to ask more questions to make the assumption less problematic. Also, if we try to combine the first agreement with the second agreement, then we will have the ability to improve our lives and come that much closer to a positive goal of happiness and understanding for others.

The third agreement is even more difficult to follow. The third agreement is "Do not take anything personally."

Wow! If everyone could have that attitude, then we would probably eliminate 90% of the disputes that exist in the world, not to mention the disputes that exist in our own lives. I know this agreement is challenging, but it really does work.

On numerous occasions I tell myself not to take things personally. When I do not take comments personally, I find that I am able to live in a blissful state of contentment. When one does not take personally what family, friends, and enemies say, then one is not stressed, and that quality of "uncommon sense" becomes evident so that one lives in peace and happiness, an attitude that is above and beyond what is anticipated. My humble opinion is that this one agreement will bring us more tranquility and contentment to our personal well-being than any of the others.

The fourth and final agreement happens to coincide with my basic philosophical belief. It is simply "Do the best you can." Again, we are all creatures of God, and each of us serves a purpose during our time here on earth. If one pursues doing the best one can, surely we will leave our world a better place.

In summarizing my philosophy in a nutshell, it is "Keep it simple and do the right thing by being impeccable with your words, not making any assumptions, not taking anything personally, and doing the best you can." When I combine this philosophy with my religious beliefs, I find them to be very complementary.

– 69 –
Nothing Is Impossible

As mentioned in an earlier chapter, the pillars of my foundation consist of faith, spirituality, education, community, and family. In that chapter I mentioned my favorite scriptures from the Bible. These scriptures have served as my guiding light throughout my lifetime and support my belief that we live in God's favor. The first scripture from Proverbs 3:5-6 states, "Trust in the Lord with all your heart and lean not upon your own understanding; acknowledge Him in all your ways and He will direct your paths." For me, this is all about loving and respecting all people. I continue to believe that God is a loving God and wants us to live in peace and happiness. We do have to live with a lot of trust.

I believe God expects us to respect all people and that respect is inclusive, not exclusive. Having respect for all people includes Protestants, Catholics, Muslims, Buddhists, and the millions of other people with different religious beliefs. This scripture speaks about trust and faith. When we speak of faith, I am reminded that if one has the faith as small as a grain of mustard seed, then nothing shall be impossible. We should be living in a world full of hope and not in a world full of fear and despair. I am certain that the possibility exists that we can all live in a better and more peaceful world.

– 70 –
Don't Live In Fear

This belief is reinforced by the second scripture that I mentioned: Philippians 4:13 which states, "I can do all things through Christ who strengthens me." These two scriptures have helped me to face the numerous challenges in the past half century, and I am confident that these same scriptures will help me in the next half century. It is because of my basic religious beliefs that I have never lived my life in fear.

When I see people living in fear today, I think it is partly due to a belief in religious exclusivity that fails to respect other people. I personally feel that religions should be inclusive and not judgmental of other people or their beliefs unless they are destructive. Our religious leaders in the world today need to show by example what they preach and work harder than the governments to create peace among all people and respect religious beliefs that are not on the path of destruction. Perhaps we need a better understanding of what it means to trust in God, especially since our national motto is "In God We Trust." I think governments should consist of religions, but that religions should not constitute governments.

"In matters of principle, stand like a rock; in matters of taste, swim with the current. Give up money, give up fame, give up science, give up earth itself and all it contains, rather than do an immoral act. And never suppose, that any situation, or under any circumstances, it is best for you to do a dishonorable thing. Whenever you are to do a thing, though it can never be known but to yourself, ask yourself how you would act were all the world looking at you, and act accordingly."

—President Thomas Jefferson

Chapter Nine
Advice for the Next Generation

– 71 –
REDUCE CORRUPTION AND INEFFICIENCY

I think many of Thomas Jefferson's principles are good guidelines to follow. One person recently quoted Thomas Jefferson in the "High Plains Journal," stating, "A government that is big enough to give everyone what they want is a government that is big enough to take everything you have." I think the future generation will have to closely monitor how much the government is controlling and how much the government is taking from the people to maintain governmental control.

In McPherson County, we have the only formal chess school in the state of Kansas. The purpose of the school is to teach life-time values such as time management, short-term planning, long-term planning, and the ability to use our brains in both the creative and analytical senses. When the new generation can analyze and be creative, then we will begin to reduce corruption and inefficiencies in government.

– 72 –
Changing Directions

After nearly twenty years, my son Layton is becoming part of that new generation that all of us will have to believe in. He is now experiencing that change in the right direction with his own set of beliefs. How did he get there?

For Layton, it was indeed a journey. My son has grown up in a society where judges or the government have made the decisions affecting him as well as decisions that affect more than 50 percent of the families in today's society. That fact is based on the number of divorces among married couples. Most of the time the children have become "entitled" by a judge's decision based on the best interests of the child as defined by the law. Unfortunately, our society made a change that went in the wrong direction by not considering the importance of the family relationships that must be preserved.

The right direction is not about living in fear of not receiving child support or child custody. The right direction is about raising a child that is respected and supported by both parents with an understanding of family values. The right direction involves education, understanding, and love that all relatives, friends, and people in our society contribute for the growth and development of all children. No child deserves to live without the freedom to explore and learn from the world that surrounds him. Slowly, our court system is changing in the right direction, but, in the last twenty years or so, our court system has been failing most children by not fully providing for their best interests.

Moving or changing in the right direction not only applies to families, but to all citizens. This is especially true when we speak of healthcare and the toleration of other races, religions, and equal rights.

– 73 –
Maintaining Family Values

We continuously reiterate that we want a government of the people, by the people, and for the people; but that should not mean a government that dictates to the people or corrupts the people. It will take a lot of hard work to maintain family values that are the foundation of our nation. It will take a lot of hard work to create a healthcare program that we can afford. It will take even more hard work to fight healthcare corruption, insurance corruption, and government corruption.

What I see in government is too much petty corruption and a great waste of taxpayers' money on issues supporting change in the wrong direction. I would like to see the next generation live a life with a standard of living and a quality of life that is better than our present generation or the past generation. This will only happen if we begin today to make the necessary changes.

– 74 –
Making the Same Mistakes

What is the right direction? Almost anyone with a small sense of history will say that the right direction means not to continue to make the same mistakes that have been made in the past. If one keeps doing the same thing the same way, one will always get the same results.

For example, more than thirty-five years ago we were warned about the problems of automobiles using excessive amounts of the earth's limited resources. Whatever happened to the creativity to solve the gas shortage crisis of 1974? I think it was a lack of foresight by the government to choose change in the right direction. Our government chose to ignore those warnings, and so did the automobile industries. I find it difficult to justify the bailout of General Motors, now known as "government motors," who ignored warnings that would have allowed them to avoid making the same mistakes because their industry failed to recognize the need for change. We need to educate the next generation on how to be forward thinkers so that they will recognize how to prevent these kinds of situations and make appropriate changes.

– 75 –
TEACH A MAN TO FISH

The long-term key to jobs and an improved economy is not continued bailouts, but improvements in educating the next generation. So, how do we educate the next generation?

One idea would be for the government to employ every high school graduate for one year in any of the federal departments of the government. For example, graduates could be given jobs with the Department of State, the Department of Energy, the Department of Defense, the Department of Housing or Education or Homeland Security. Let our youth see first-hand the abundant waste in these massive government bureaucracies and become educated in how to improve government agencies.

Another idea is to promote quarterly semesters at our colleges and vocational schools so that these facilities are fully used in a cost effective and beneficial manner. Not only will higher education be more efficient, but today's generation will have the opportunity to get more education in less time and then become a productive asset for our society. We do not need to become a welfare state. We should be able to choose and make a choice to move in the right direction.

With education will come jobs and with good education will come less corruption. I can only speculate that with less corruption, there will be less bureaucracy and inefficiencies in government. As an old Chinese proverb states, "Give a man a fish and you feed him for a day. Teach a man to fish and you feed him for a lifetime." We need to emphasize the importance of better teaching to have better-educated citizens. If our next generation is going to be better than the last great generation, then we had better start today to make changes in the right direction. That is the kind of change I can believe in. Change that I can believe in does not involve giving everyone a handout.

– 76 –
Helping Others

I know a few students who understand and live by this philosophy. They are extremely motivated and are willing to help others learn to learn. I would encourage more people to establish more endowments to our institutions of higher learning so that our next generation will gain more knowledge. Then, that new generation with more knowledge and understanding will have the ability to make our communities better for all generations.

If one wishes to improve jobs and economy, then one must make changes in the right direction. The short-term answer may be to keep the financial system, the banks and insurance companies stabilized, but that is not the long-term answer. By long-term I am talking about the next twenty to twenty-five years. Long-term will be sometime in the next generation. What is needed is not change we can believe in, but a new generation that we can believe in. That involves helping others to learn.

We still have the opportunity to choose to make a change in the right direction. For the past 234 years we have survived because we had perseverance and leadership to continue to change in the right direction. We must have more perseverance and good leadership if we are going to be here for another 234 years.

Success

To laugh often and much; to win the respect of intelligent people and affection of children; to earn the appreciation of honest critics and endure the betrayal of false friends; to appreciate beauty, to find the best in others; to leave the world a bit better, whether by a healthy child, a garden patch or a redeemed social condition; to know even one life has breathed easier because you have lived. This is to have succeeded.

—Ralph Waldo Emerson

Chapter Ten
The Golden Years

– 77 –
Life-long Values

My story would not be complete if I did not reflect on the present and what I would like to enjoy when I become thirty years older. What I would like to become is the kind of person that my dad portrays. I have been able to be active with my dad in his golden years by giving back some of the life-long values that he has given to me, such as respect and understanding. I want to give a few recent examples of how life can still be exciting, rewarding, and adventuresome as one enters that ninth decade of life.

– 78 –
Beauty and Peace

Two years ago my dad and I made what has become our annual trip to Tucson, Arizona, to visit his nephew and family. We usually leave with an early morning start and begin the drive from Galva to Hutchinson and Pratt with a stop for gas in Liberal in southwestern Kansas. As we drive through Greensburg on the way to Liberal, we notice the massive rebuilding from the tornado that literally flattened that community in 2007. It is inspiring to see the new construction that shows the resilience of these people who are dedicated to rebuilding their community. In this part of Kansas the terrain is much flatter, and one can see for miles and miles. My dad always comments on how far one can see in all directions on a clear day. He talks about the beauty of the crops and the peacefulness of the grazing cattle.

From Liberal we drive through the panhandle of Oklahoma, then through a small portion of Texas and stop for gas and dinner in Tucumcari, New Mexico, on old Route 66. We especially enjoy the Mexican cuisine at the Thunderbird Lodge. After a nice rest, we continue our drive on Interstate-40 all the way to Albuquerque, where we spend the night.

– 79 –
Time for Eating

The next morning we usually stop for breakfast at our favorite Mexican restaurant and begin the final half of our journey to Tucson, traveling down Interstate-25 to the small village of Hatch, New Mexico, the "Chile Capital of the World," where we have a chile hamburger for lunch at Sparky's Restaurant. It is a "must stop" for anyone traveling on the shortcut from Interstate-25 to Interstate-10.

The remainder of the trip goes fast on the interstate, and we arrive at my dad's nephew's home just in time for a big dinner. It is the family atmosphere with Frank and Connie Wicks that makes the whole trip a total success. During our visit, we also meet many other friends and family.

Thanksgiving 2008 at the home of Frank and Connie Wicks.

– 80 –
California Adventure

On our visit two years ago, we traveled farther west to Los Angeles, California, to visit with my dad's grandson (my nephew) Robert and his wife Nicole. We continued our journey to Merced, California, to visit one of my dad's childhood friends and boxing buddy from Galva, Red Matthes, and his wife Roberta. Just watching Red and my dad talk about the old days when they were boxing, dating, and going to school was inspiring. It was a picture of two men who, during their middle years of life, had served their country in World War II and raised a family while remaining the closest of friends.

Our next stop was in San Francisco, which was near Hamilton Air Force Base, where my dad had been assigned after the war. He was one of only two pilots to fly General "Hap" Arnold, a five-star general. General Arnold remains the first and, as of this writing more that 50 years later, the only five-star general of the United States Air Force. We celebrated the New Year in California with friends and then made the long trip back to Kansas.

It was a wonderful and memorable adventure. It is my hope, that when I am living in my ninth decade, I can look forward to trips like these with my son and share such treasured moments and adventures.

– 81 –
Music and Dancing Fish

This past year, we spent more time in Arizona with Frank and Connie and made a special visit to the Tucson Museum's Arts and Crafts Festival. My dad has always enjoyed music, especially playing the guitar and the harmonica. The Arts and Crafts Festival was made to order for my dad because the museum had many talented local entertainers who played folk and country music in the warmth of the outdoor performance area.

While enjoying a wonderful time with my dad and relatives, I was able to enjoy the displays of arts and crafts and found an intricate metal sculpture called "Dancing Fish." The sculptor Jorge Gonzalez was selling several of his works at his booth at the festival. He was visiting the Studio at the Sculpture Resource Center in Tucson and was represented by the Azora Gallery. The tools that were used to create his sculpture had been made in his dad's shop in Manizales, Colombia.

Dancing Fish by Jorge Gonzalez.

Since my birth month is represented by Pisces, it was only fitting that I would be attracted to the beauty of the "Dancing Fish." This is another example of how the interactions of family and friends throughout the world can share and enjoy the God-given talents that inspire and create new ideas. The "Dancing Fish" represents the fascinating free movement of the fish in their adventurous water world.

– 82 –
The Song Fest

After a few hours at the Arts and Crafts Festival, we visited the home of one of the local entertainers who were close friends of Frank and Connie. Kevin Hughes and his wife, Trina invited us to listen to Kevin and his colleague Peter Ott perform a variety of country songs on their guitars. They had an extra guitar which my dad played, and, as a trio, they performed most admirably. Dad definitely enjoyed the song fest. Kevin, a nurse, and Peter, a heart-surgeon, are entertainers known as the "RuffMixx." They sing acoustic country blues as a hobby when they are not working in the hospital.

– 83 –
East Coast Adventure

In addition to the annual visit to Tucson, Dad and I made a trip a few weeks earlier to the East Coast to visit another friend and World War II veteran in Virginia.

Bill Price and my dad had shared many experiences after World War II when they and their families were both assigned to Japan.

During our trip to the east coast, Dad and I visited the new Air Force Memorial in Washington, D.C., and the new World War II Memorial. Everywhere we walked, we noticed that all of the visitors to these memorials showed enormous respect for veterans who had served to defend the principles upon which our nation was founded. It is my hope that the younger generations can view these memorials and learn from the history that they represent.

Marck and Redell at WW II Memorial, Washington, D.C.

May you find serenity and tranquility in a world you may not always understand. May the pain you have known and the conflict you have experienced give you the strength to walk through life facing each new situation with courage and optimism. Always know that there are those whose love and understanding will always be there, even when you feel most alone. May you discover enough goodness in others to believe in a world of peace. May a kind word, a reassuring touch, and a warm smile be yours every day of your life, and may you give these gifts as well as receive them. Remember the sunshine when the storm seems unending. Teach love to those who hate, and let that love embrace you as you go out into the world. May the teachings of those you admire become part of you, so that you may call upon them. Remember, those whose lives you have touched and whose have touched yours are always a part of you, even if the encounters were less than you would have wished. It is the content of the encounter that is more important than the form. May you not become too concerned with material matters, but instead place immeasurable value on the goodness in your heart. Find time each day to see beauty and love in the world around you. Realize that each person has limitless abilities, but each of us is different in our own way. What you feel you lack in the present may become one of your strengths in the future. May you see your future as one filled with promise and possibility. Learn to view everything as a worthwhile experience. May you find enough inner strength to determine your own worth by yourself, and not be dependent on another's judgment of your accomplishments. May you always feel loved.

—Unknown

Epilogue

This book is based on my personal experiences, acquaintances, and relationships with individuals and their creative arts. It is about finding hope and inspiration from the interaction of people with people and our environment. It involves the cultural awareness and learning about the natural beauty that surrounds us and creates peace and harmony.

What is the significance of uncommon sense? Uncommon sense is the ability to create a synergistic effect, where the whole is greater than the sum of its parts by combining the natural qualities of the earth with the natural born talents of the individuals who inhabit the earth. Uncommon sense allows us to become inspired and motivated by the understanding of nature and man's need to live in this world. The individual must learn to respect our natural environment to create a balance that is mutually beneficial for the present and the future.

In our world today we see one attempt at accomplishing this goal by the ideas of the individuals pushing the concepts of the "green movement" to improve the environment. In the past we have seen our country striving for this goal by preserving natural lands and endangered species. The idea of uncommon sense is to use our education and knowledge to develop the ability to improve our quality and standard of living while preserving the balance of nature to insure a world that will allow future generations to live and prosper in a healthy and peaceful environment.

All too often governments try to take extreme measures in one direction or the other. Either the government starts destroying nature without any regard to the long-term impact, such as the destruction of the rain forests in South America, or the government ignores the needs of the population to use the natural resources for development and allows nature to remain unused, such as not developing land in Africa to become more productive for growing crops.

Uncommon sense dictates that we need to work together by learning and respecting the contributions that every human has to offer. Our challenge is to work for the common good, attain the knowledge to make wise decisions, to learn from our experiences, and to develop our lives in a constructive and peaceful manner.

Uncommon sense uses everything that is available to make changes in the right direction. Changes in the right direction are not about building walls and creating exclusive areas of good or bad. Instead, uncommon sense is about breaking down barriers and creating more inclusive areas that create greater opportunities for the good of all mankind. It is our mandate to strive for this goal and

Epilogue

to recognize that we live in a small world that must be shared in a respectful manner that allows positive growth for everyone.

This book is about the uncommon sense that I have perceived over the more than sixty years of my life. This book is meant to provide meaning to life, to inspire others to use their God-given talents, to respect and understand the contributions made by man and nature, to learn from our experience, and to provide a philosophy and belief that leads to peace and harmony.

About the Author

Marck Cobb has served as a licensed attorney for the state of Kansas for the past twenty years. His most recent past experience has been as a legal mediator to facilitate "win-win" solutions for domestic and civil law issues. He has been involved in leadership positions with the American Red Cross Sunflower Chapter in McPherson, Kansas; the International Chess Institute of the Midwest in Lindsborg, Kansas; the McPherson Museum and Arts Foundation, the McPherson Chamber of Commerce, and the McPherson County Bar Association.

He served for twenty-four years with the U.S. Air Force in the defense of our nation and retired as Lieutenant Colonel. He served as a command pilot, diplomat, and Pentagon analyst. He negotiated an international treaty for special flight operations between the United States and the former Soviet Union.

As Deputy Chief for Long-Range Planning for the Air Force in the Pentagon, he supervised the air operation research plans for the first Gulf War. Cobb has been awarded the Distinguished Flying Cross, the Air Medal, the Defense Meritorious Service Medal, and other medals for his flying achievements in Southeast Asia, his diplomacy in Russia, and his accomplishments in the Pentagon.

Cobb is a graduate of Galva Rural High School, Galva, Kansas; the U.S. Air Force Academy, Colorado; the Naval Postgraduate School, Monterey, California; and Washburn University Law School, Topeka, Kansas. He lives in Galva, Kansas and is married to Francine. His son, Layton, is an Eagle Scout and sophomore at Wichita State University. Presently, Cobb is a candidate for United States Representative from the First Congressional District in Kansas.